# Prejudice Within Your Race

Esther Myhan and Lucille Allensworth

authorHOUSE®

*AuthorHouse*™
*1663 Liberty Drive*
*Bloomington, IN 47403*
*www.authorhouse.com*
*Phone: 1-800-839-8640*

*First published by AuthorHouse 10/8/2009*

*ISBN: 978-1-4490-2809-1 (sc)*
*ISBN: 978-1-4490-2810-7 (hc)*
*ISBN: 978-1-4490-2811-4 (e)*

*Printed in the United States of America*
*Bloomington, Indiana*

*This book is printed on acid-free paper.*

# Acknowledgement

We would like to acknowledge and thank all
the contributors for their willingness to share their
personal and often painful experiences with us,
without which, there would not even be a book.
We would also like to thank Dr. Shagufta Jabeen,
Professor at Meharry Medical College Department of
Psychiatry & Behavioral Science in Nashville, Tennessee
for her time and efforts in her contributions to the book.

We would also like to thank our editors Robert
Allensworth and Jim Myhan for their hard work
and support in completing this book. We also
want to thank them for believing in what we were
trying to accomplish by writing this book, a
desire to make others aware of the problems of
of prejudice within your own race. We hope by
making others aware of this problem, we might
start to eliminate the prejudice we have with one another.

# Contents

# Introduction

There are so many things, so many reasons that led us to put this book together. Many personal experiences, from things we heard at the beauty salon, to things our children came home and told us they heard, negative things that are said about both dark skinned and light skinned blacks. We could not believe these things still went on in this day and time (2008). Many of the things that haunted us for so long, things we thought were healed within us, we realized were not resolved when brought to our attention again. Our hope is that when you read this book, it brings to life some of the hurtful things that are being said, why they are being said, and how we can move on from this. We need to forgive each other as our Heavenly father forgives us. Let's look deep inside ourselves and ask questions. Let's talk about the issue and if we find ourselves still struggling, let this be a beginning to our healing. These issues go all the way back to slavery, or could it have started with Cain and Abel?

After conducting some preliminary research, we found that not only our black brothers and sisters but others also have been singled out, stereotyped, made to feel different because of ethnicity, height, religion, hair color, etc… And though other books may cover similar territory, these are our stories and events, and those of our friends, family, and acquaintances.

Dr. Shagufta Jabeen a Professor at Meharry Medical College in Nashville, Tennessee whose studies include "Behavior Disorder," will be the final contributor to our book, and will shine some light on the subject of prejudice, its causes and consequences.

Please listen to the professional and what she has to say about it. Let's begin now, kick your feet up, get a cup of coffee or tea or beverage of choice, and enjoy reading "Prejudice Within Your Race."

Song of Solomon

How right they are to adore you!!!!dark am I yet lovely
O daughter of Jerusalem dark light the tents of Kadar.

# Esther's Story

"You think you are pretty because you are light skinned"….that was the most ridiculous one of them all! I hated my skin color as much as they did. "I think I am very ugly" was my response in my head, but because I was too afraid to say anything, nothing came out of my mouth.

I didn't think I was better or prettier than any one else. Do I think I received better treatment from people when I was young because of my skin color? I guess I would have to say no to that question. I would like to think much of what I received or achieved in my youth, like being the head majorette of my high school band, was due to my hard work and extra effort. When I was head majorette, I did not choose all light skinned girls like me; I chose a variety of other girls, girls whose color was light brown to very dark. I chose the other majorettes based on their ability to march and twirl, not the tone of their skin.

I was the only 8th grader to have been chosen that year to be a majorette in the high school band, and it was not because I was light skinned. They said it had to do with the way I walk: "You walk like you are marching and it would not be hard to train you." So, when I look back on this now, I am grateful and feel it was something I earned. Both of the head majorettes that year that selected me were very brown skinned girls, not light skinned like me. I was hated by many of the other girls since I was the only 8th grader chosen for the squad, many times they would even try to start fights with me. I felt nothing but hate from so many of the other girls I grew up with. The more I tried to befriend them, the more they hated me. I thought I had one real friend, but even she would do and say cruel things to me. All I wanted was to be her friend, and at times I felt like she was my best friend. "Why do you treat me that way?" I asked her, she said: "I don't know" (she was dark skinned). How sad is that?

I have been called pecan-tan, high yellow, white girl, half breed and many others most of my life. I've been called these names by my own siblings as well as the other children I went to school with. I was really hurt by most of the name calling. I did not choose my skin color, why hate me because of it? I remember a story my mother told me when I was young. She said that when I was born she could hear the nurses whispering about us, saying that I must be a white man's child. My mother is brown skinned; some would say chocolate or cocoa. The whispering went on until my father got to the hospital then they knew that I was his child. My father was a very light skinned black man (my father's mother was bi-racial, her mother was white). I remember my father telling us a story about when black people had to ride on the back of the bus, he said he never did! He said he did not pretend to be white, he just never did, and because he looked white no one questioned him about it.

Most of the friends I made were people of my complexion or a little darker. I always hated my complexion. I actually was very envious of my dark skinned sisters and the other dark skinned girls I knew. I thought they were the most beautiful people in the whole world. So I would do everything I could to try to become darker, from lying in the sun to wearing dark make-up, but nothing worked. I would get a little darker from being out in the sun in the spring and summer months, but in the winter I would lose the tan and become pale and light complexioned again. I always thought I was the most unattractive person in my family.

Unlike many other light skinned blacks, I have always been attracted to men of many different races. I have dated black men from Africa as well as Caucasian men, race or color never bothered me that way. However, I have always thought that dark skinned black men are the most beautiful men in God's world. When I was a child, I remember hearing a story that said drinking coffee would turn you black. So, I began drinking coffee at an early age and was very disappointed when I never saw any change in my complexion.

Every year I tried out for and got roles in my school's plays, I really enjoyed these activities. Many of the other kids would say I got the roles because I was "light skinned". I would ask these kids if they tried out for a part in the play and they would say no. I rest my case! I didn't get a role in the play because of my skin tone; it was because I made the effort to try-out for the part. The school plays characters were chosen for their talent and acting ability. In fact, if memory serves me correct, I was usually the only light skinned person in the play.

These are just a few of the things I went through while growing up, there are many stories like these. When we were interviewing people for this book, I interviewed one of my dark skinned sisters who is very beautiful. I always thought she looked how I thought an angel must look. I really looked up to her even though she was one of the siblings who would call me names. She said when she was in junior high school, she ran for Miss Alton Park and came in as first runner up. She said she didn't win even though she had much more talent than the "high yellow girl" that won. This was later confirmed by one or more of her teachers, the other girl had won not because she was prettier or had more talent, but simply because she was "high yellow".

I never thought my brother-in-law Julius would have a story to tell, but he did. Julius said that when he was young he felt like an outcast because everyone else in his family, mother and sisters, were all light skinned. He said he was not treated differently, but somehow he just always felt different. Julius said he never understood these feelings until he came to the south and met his father for the first time. His father was a dark skinned man and this explained his own color, now he understood. Julius also said he had always been attracted to light skinned women; he credits this to his first love, his mother.

It took me a long time to love who I am, flaws and all. However, the damage that was done to me years ago was very hurtful, and took time for me to overcome.

In writing my story, and the stories of others whom I interviewed, I hope we can be healed from the jealousy and hatred mentioned in these stories.

I wish we could all rejoice in our differences and love one another unconditionally. We know that prejudice will be around until Jesus comes back, but if we can help one person by publishing this book then it will all be worth it. Let me say to all my dark skinned and light skinned sisters, love who you are, never think anyone is any better than you. We are all God's children; let's put an end to self hatred, and hatred of others who look different than us.

Finally accepting and satisfied
With who I am, in His name
Esther

## Keisha's Story

My mother told me that she really didn't experience any issues as a child. Although her complexion was lighter than that of her siblings, her aunt treated each of them the same. It was when her aunt sent her to New York when she was a teenager that she became more aware of her color. Her relatives in New York would always say: "You think you're something because you got that skin color on you!" She said she didn't put much stock in that statement at the time because there were other issues in the family that she was dealing with.

All of her adult life she's been attracted to darker skinned men. She said she thought men her color and lighter were weak. Her marriage to my father brought a new dynamic to the color issue, being darker skinned, he was teased a lot as a kid. Because of his dark complexion, my dad was called "buck wheat." My dad carried this complex into his adult life. At times when he would go into an establishment and have to talk to a light skinned person, he would walk away feeling like he had been talked down too. In his mind, lighter skinned people "got over" (had it easier) because of their color and darker skinned people had to have an education and money to make it.

When my parents moved to New York, my dad felt as if people were judging him because he had married a light skinned woman. He felt people thought that my mom was making a fool out of him; that he was a fool because he married that light skinned woman. My dad would send her into places where she could use her color to "get over." For example, if they couldn't pay a bill, he would send mom in to get an extension because he felt the white people would respond better to her. My mom admits she was "color struck" (she had a color preference), but as she's gotten older she realizes that people are people regardless of color.

My dad still has a complex to a certain extent, but he's gotten better as he's gotten older. About 10 years ago, I started dating a guy while I was in college and he was a light skinned man. My dad didn't like him at first sight.

My mom later told me that my dad made a comment about the guy's complexion. But a few years later when I met my husband, my father liked him, and his skin tone is light also. I realize that personality is a factor, but I also attribute this change to my dad moving past those old complexes. But I will say to this day, when my parents argue, they always find a way to mention each other's color.

# My Caucasian Sister

I am a white woman with natural blonde hair and very blue eyes. I've had to struggle with certain issues all my life, like blond jokes; people think I am very ignorant because I am blonde! I have an MBA in Accounting and a minor in Business. I work for a major corporation and have a six figure salary. I achieved all this through hard work, although some people think I got where I am because I slept my way to the top. I am sure there are some blondes out there (brunettes, red heads & raven-haired beauties) where this preconceived impression may be true, but that's not how I got to be where I am. So, please stop stereotyping all blondes as dumb, I am very offended by it. Men need to stop trying to come on to me or get me into bed because they think I am easy; men should talk to me, get to know me, and they will learn I am an intelligent woman with lots to offer. Please stop calling me "Barbie," I can't help the way I look; I will not dye my hair as many have suggested, just to be taken seriously.

# Sisters

As a child, I remember sitting in my daddy's lap with my sister giving me the evil eye. My daddy would say things that were cruel, but at the time, I did not think of them that way. As an adult thinking back, I have had to face some issues and deal with them. Also, it makes me realize just how much at fault my father was in the on-going relationship problems between my sister and me, and that he was a very prejudiced man. He treated my sister differently. Oh, he loved her in his on way I suppose, but it was very unhealthy for the relationship between my sister and me. I was daddy's favorite and he did not mind letting me and the whole world know it! I got more toys than my sister, more of his time than she did, and in my mind this was all because I was good and never got into trouble like my sister did. We fought all the time, she would get a spanking but I wouldn't.

My sister and I have been estranged for many years. We are civil toward each other, but are very much divided. I had not wanted to face the reasons why until my children started doing some of the same things that we did. I have two daughters who are very different and I started to see them behave so much like my sister and me that I had to face up to a lot of things. I had to put an end to this prejudice among us; I did not want them to be like the two of us. We, my sister and I, are working on our relationship as well. We are so grateful to offer our story in the hopes that we can help someone else stop the hate. Don't let your lives be ruined by such behavior; after all, we are all God's children.

# Red Headed and Loving It

The story you just read is my sisters. Yes, I hated her for years, but I am so very happy to announce that not only are we working on our relationship, but our children are as well. She stated before how I was treated differently than she; the hurt I experienced as a result, was not about the number of toys, I did not receive, it was the lack of love from my father. The way my father treated me was terrible! He called me his "red headed devil" because my temper would always get me into trouble. I am sure you have heard the stories of red heads and their tempers. I was such an angry child because my father treated my sister better than me, and my mother stood by and allowed it to happen!

I wish I could say that we reconciled before my father passed away, but we didn't. I tried reaching out to him on more than one occasion, but it got to be too painful. I asked him why he was so resentful, why he didn't love me. He said: "I did love you.....I fed, clothed you, kept a roof over your head, and I made sure you had a good education, even though you kept defying me and being friends with ni...rs" (he used the "N" word). I told him that even thought he tried to teach us that we are the superior race, and are better than any other, I never bought into it. I told him that maybe I felt this way because he had treated me different from my sister. I am very sad that my father never got to know me, but I realize it was his loss, not mine. I am more saddened by the fact that he never received Jesus Christ as his savior, so we won't even meet again because of it. Loving Christ as I do, I learned to forgive my father and my mother who, by-the way- is very much alive today and recognizes her part in the way we were brought up. My mother is truly sorry and my sister and I both forgive her for this and love the way things are now. The first step we took was going to a diversity seminar hosted by one of the authors. We thought it was going to be about understanding other races. Little did we know when we attended the seminar it was going to not only be about other races, but also about facing some of the facts about our on race and each other, how we are different and how to embrace those differences with love and respect for each other. I am very grateful for this book being printed; yes there are other ones out there, but none like this one. It has been very healing to just talk and tell this story. My sister and I are very happy to have this chance.

Love & Respect
Red Headed and Loving it

# Shine
## Attorney At Law

I knew him even before the introductions were made. When he walked in the restaurant his very presence captivated me. We stood as he strolled across the room toward us, why we stood I'm still not sure; it's not like he was royalty, but at the time it felt like it for just a moment. He looked at us as he approached. He is dark as the night with baby smooth skin and teeth as white as snow. He is so perfectly formed, with just a touch of grey at his temples which only added to his good looks. When I tore my eyes away from the beauty of this man God created, I glanced around the room and noticed not one, but several sets of eyes on him. The women all had smiles on their faces. He looked to be about 6 feet 2 inches tall as I focused on the man in front of me while the introductions were made. With all the professionalism I could muster, I explained to him about the tape recorder and the project I was working on. I asked if he had a story to tell, would he be willing to share it with me? The following is his story.

You see, hate for me started with my parents, who treated me and my sister differently. While she stayed when company came over, I was asked to go play in my room. At the time, I did not understand what was going on; I just thought they like her better than me. I did not equate it with color, not then (she is lighter complexioned than me).

One day I overheard my parents talking about how one of them missed out on a job because of a light skinned black and how sick and tired they were that these things kept happening over and over again. Oh how they hated light skinned people, and how light skinned people thought they were better than the rest of us. They would go on and on like this for hours and it would only stop when my sister was at home. I started to dislike her because I could not understand why mom and dad treated her better than me if they felt this way about light skinned blacks.

I was so confused at that point; I would pick on my sister all the time. When she got picked on at school by other kids, I would never take up for her, because I felt the same way they did. I started fights with all light skinned dudes just for the heck of it. These guys did nothing to me; they were just the wrong color, sound familiar? Also, the fact that most girls seemed to like the light skinned dudes better didn't help things. But as I got older, things changed, I found there was no shortage of girls, dark or light, who were interested in me. However, I would respect and treat the dark skinned girl's great, but treated the light skinned girls the total opposite. I treated them like dogs, not like women at all. This went on for quite some time, and for this I am forever ashamed.

I like to think that things changed for me when I received Jesus Christ as my savior, yes that was the start of getting rid of the old for something new and clean.

But not until I faced my parents and told them respectfully the harm they did to me, and how I forgave them, did I really start to get better and was able to begin to forgive myself. Also, I had to start to build a relationship with my sister. I tried to find all the women that had crossed my path and tell them how sorry I was for what I done to them.

Now this, my final step in healing, putting all of this on paper hoping it will help someone else with what ever prejudice they may have.

As I watch Barack Obama run for president, my question is, if he was a dark skinned black man, would he have the support that he has? I mean, if he had two dark skinned parents would he have been as successful? Now, don't get me wrong. I hope the brother wins, not only because he is black, but because I feel it's time for a change. But the question remains.

As I close, I am remembering two of my favorite poems by Langston Hughes:

"I, Too, Sing America." I am the darker brother, they send me to eat in the kitchen when company comes, but I laugh and eat well and grow strong. Tomorrow I'll be at the table when company comes nobody'll dare say to me, eat in the kitchen, then. Besides, they'll see how beautiful I am and be ashamed. I too am America.

"Dream Variations" To fling my arms wide in some place of the sun, to whirl and to dance till the white day is done. Then rest at cool evening beneath a tall tree while night comes on gently, dark like me. That is my dream! To fling my arms wide in the face of the sun, dance, whirl, whirl, till the quick day is done. Rest at pale evening, a tall, slim tree. Night coming tenderly, black like me.

Forever Black
Shine

# Bright as Light, M.D.

"You have skin that is bright, be proud of the light, and let your love shine through!" This is what I would hear from my mother all the time when I would come home complaining about what someone had said about my light skin. I was even hated among some of the young brothers I grew up with; some made jokes about me and treated me harshly. People always made me feel as though I was different when all I wanted was to belong. My little sister once said someone told her that a lot of light skinned guys are gay, she then asked me: "Does that mean you are?" This craziness has to stop; there was nothing feminine about me!

I finally came into my on when I stopped letting others tell me what is real and what is not, when I stopped letting others get to me with what they had to say. Sadly, it took me getting older to realize that people will say and do things because they are jealous, or have problems themselves. These people chose to attack me instead of trying to figure out why they felt the way they did in the first place. However, before I finally came to this realization, the damage had been done. If I had not had a strong and loving family that gave me much support, I hate to think where I would be today.

Whoever you are reading these personal accounts of prejudice in the lives of others, read these recollections not for enjoyment, but for a lesson we need to learn. We all need to be careful how we treat people in our race and those of other races. The tongue is a sharp tool that can cause much damage and do much harm to others. Allow me to close by saying to the authors of this book, thank you for telling my story. I hope my story can help stop some of the prejudice within our race and other races as well.

We can be a strong race if we learn to band together and love each other. We need to accept each other and embrace our differences.

Yes, my skin is bright, and my light did not always shine through, but I succeeded in spite of what others said.

Bright as Light M.D.

# Blackberry

I am a dark skinned sister who is very comfortable within her on skin. I don't dislike now, nor have I ever, anyone of my black sisters of a different tone or complexion. We are all very beautiful, we just have different skin tones, and this is what makes us unique. I think it's very petty and sad that some of us still struggle with these issues. I know how it all started and why it started, but its time to move beyond the past! We need to love each other as God loves us. Imagine how strong we would be if we stood together, unified, one race. How powerful we would be, a force to be reckoned with. I know there are other books out there about prejudice, but this book is different, as all voices are allowed to be heard. I want to thank you for this opportunity, I hope the millions of people who read this will be able to move forward and be healed from your efforts.

Lots of Love
Blackberry.

# Sunshine

I am 28 years old, my parents are light skinned. I was asked many times in high school if I was biracial; it always irritated me for some reason. I would answer no of course, both my parents are black. They would say: "you are really beautiful; you look mixed with your hazel eyes." I would answer that my grandmother, who is dark skinned, has blue eyes. I guess that's where I got my eye color. They would look at me like I was making this up or something.

If you asked me if I struggle with my color, I would say no. However, I used to live in tanning salons in the winter and outside in the sun in the summer. If you asked me what type of man I prefer, I would have to say brown to dark skinned men. What I would like to say in this interview is that I would like someone to like me for me, not what they see on the outside, but what's on the inside. Don't tell me I am beautiful just because of the color of my eyes or the color of my skin. Tell me I'm beautiful because you've taken the time to get to know me and love me for who I am as a person, a person who loves God with all of her heart. Tell me I'm beautiful because of the way I treat people, not because of my external features. True beauty is not the color of someone's skin or eye color, or even the texture of their hair. True beauty is found by what's on the inside of a person.

Thanks for the opportunity,

Sunshine

# German, Trinidadian or Other

My father's family came to the New York area from the island of Trinidad. Of course slave ships brought slaves from Africa to the Caribbean Islands to farm the sugar cane plantations which were needed to satisfy Europe's desire for this sweet spice. The people of Trinidad today vary in complexion due to generations of descendents of these slaves mating with native peoples as well and the other foreign settlers of the islands (such as Spanish, Portuguese, French, etc).

My father's family was light skinned, but their hair texture was very "nappy" (course). So, my father's family would be considered more of African descent, not Hispanic. In the New York area today there are large populations of people of both Hispanic and African decent. People from island countries such as Trinidad may have both Hispanic and African bloodlines, but I guess the hair texture and possibly some facial features may be used to determine if someone is African American or Hispanic American.

My racial identity gets even further complicated. My father served in the U.S. Army and was stationed in Germany just after World War II, it was there that he met and married my mother. This of course was an interracial marriage in the early 50's and was not widely accepted. My mother was 100% German and 100% white. My older brother and I were both born in Germany, but later we moved to Brooklyn, NY when my father's military service was completed. My parents had 5 children and we grew-up and went to school in Brooklyn, near my father's family.

We were all light skinned, but had hair texture more typical of other African Americans. Our hair grew longer, but was always difficult to manage. We were made fun of by the other kids in our neighborhood and at school. They would call us "Whiggers." Whigger came from combining the words "White and Nigger." Such words really hurt; we just wanted to be friends. Eventually these kids became our friends, once they got to know us. We ended-up spending much time in each others homes, but I will always remember being called a "whigger."

I always found it very difficult to fill-out legal forms where there was a block for race. You had to pick one box: White, Black, Native American, and Asian Other.

If I chose Black I felt I was putting my mother down. If I chose White, I was not acknowledging my father's family. I guess I was OTHER?

OTHER?

# Kids Can Be Cruel

As a child growing up you experience many things from kids who want to be like you, to others who want to out do you. We had a neighbor whose daughter Peggy was very dark skinned. I thought she was special because of her beautiful silky dark skin, wavy hair and a sweet smile. But she had problems with another kid in the neighborhood, Jackie who picked on her a lot because of her skin color. Jackie was brown-skinned and very mean to Peggy. She would pick on her and call her names like blackie which would make Peggy cry and feel bad about herself. When I would stand up for Peggy, Jackie would say mean things to me and tell me: "You think you are white don't you?" I am light complexioned. This happened quite often until one day my mother overheard her bashing us, and went to have a heart-to-heart talk with Jackie's mom. We never had any more trouble with her. We came to realize that Jackie had personal problems of her own, but not until later in life.

My mother who is dark skinned said that this type of thing happens sometimes when children hear their parents talking that way.

I remember once attending an all black gathering and felt that I was somehow out of place. At the table in front of ours there were seated six women and two men. I noticed the ladies were staring at me and whispering, so I looked at myself wondering if something was out of place. Then I thought: "oh yes, my color, they think I must think I am better than they are." I've been told this by others just because I am of a lighter color than they are; what a sad commentary on our people. This is a common occurrence with some light complexioned people.

In the past, the black race especially, has had problems with one another in reference to skin tones. Some lighter skinned people feel that they are better or more attractive than darker skinned people; as for myself, I've never felt that way. As I said before, my mother is dark skinned but my father was of a very light complexion.

During slavery the white masters, more often than not, had the darker skinned slaves work out in the fields and the lighter slaves in the house.

This lighter verses darker treatment has been passed down from generation to generation and is present in our society even to this day. The sad thing is that we as a people perpetuate this type of stigma among ourselves.

# Tall and Different

Jennifer, who is Latino, grew up in the United States. All throughout her life she had problems with her looks. Some Latinos would laugh and check with her for being very tall and thin. While the average Latino woman's height is any where from 5'1 to 5'4, Jennifer is 5'11. Kids called her names like "string bean," but the one name she hated most of all was "Olive Oyl," the name of a cartoon character, who was the girlfriend of "Popeye the Sailor Man." Calling Jennifer "Olive Oyl" made her feel bad and sometimes made her cry. Kids can be very cruel at times. As she grew up she never wore high heels, hoping not to be laughed at but some people still stared and laughed at her.

I am sure if you were to ask her now if she has gotten over the humiliation she would say yes, that she has moved on.

Jennifer said, although she was jeered and laughed at while growing up, she feels she has overcome all the negativity she endured, and that the whole ordeal has made her into the strong woman she is today.

# Big Blue Eyes
## Kao

Kao, who is Korean, has big blue eyes. This is very unusual among oriental people but Kao Kim is one of the few.

When Kao got her first corporate job, she had no problems with people outside of her race, only from some Koreans who attended church with her would say: "how you lucked out like that having blue eyes?" Her corporate job only lasted a few years; she had to leave and go to work for her father in the cleaning business. She was hesitant at first but soon changed her mind because she knew her father needed her. Kao worked the register at her father's business; she was stared at quite often and sometimes asked how she got her blue eyes? She would say; "I ordered them," and laugh. Rumors got out saying that her father was someone other than her biological father, that she was adopted. This angered her, and she never found out who put this awful lie out but nevertheless she realized some people from her own race would make her feel like an outcast, she would sometimes say they are just jealous.

She is now working for herself and not allowing people to hurt her by staring, whispering making her feel different. What she feels is that she is special because of her looks.

# Do Blonde's Have More Fun?

I am sure that most people have heard the saying, "Blondes have more fun," or told the latest blonde joke to a co-worker or friend. For better or worse, being a blonde comes with certain assumptions in our society. I was born with blonde hair, hazel eyes and fair skin into a family of Irish and Danish descent and it was not until I heard my first "dumb blonde" joke that I realized that I was in any way different from my sister, the only dark haired child among my 4 siblings. Who knew something as simple as the color of my hair would have such an affect on how people made assumptions about my intelligence or morals, or lack thereof?

Whether people realize it or not, blondes are typically stereotyped as ditzy, flaky, unintelligent and promiscuous. Although I was the Valedictorian of my high school graduating class, I was called the "smartest dumb blonde" people had ever met on more than one occasion. And to be honest, for much of my teen-aged life, I carried that title around as a badge of honor. It wasn't until I graduated from college and entered the real world that I realized how much my looks were being perceived by those around me.

Whether I was being told I looked more "like a beauty contestant" than a viable candidate for a job during an interview or brushed off by a guy I was interested in because he didn't "normally date blondes," I quickly became aware of how my coloring was influencing the events in my life. I typically ignored the whispered comments I heard from other women about how I looked or acted that always included the statement: "Well, she's a blonde…"As if pointing out the color of my hair would somehow explain everything about my situation or me. However, it does not mean that I was not both perplexed and hurt by the attitudes I felt were unfairly cast towards me without anything more than rush judgments and stereotypes.

I am sure there are people that consider me fortunate to enter the world as I did, with long blonde hair and alabaster skin. And in no way do I mean to equate the experiences in my life to the blatant discrimination I know others have experienced. Nevertheless, I do think that all people deserve the right to be judged for their actions and deeds and not for their outward appearance.

Authors Comment:

Krista is tall, beautiful and blonde, and to some people it automatically makes her a card carrying, dues paying member of the "dumb blondes club." She is loving, educated, very intellectual and smart, and has a master's degree in genetics. Does this sound like a dummy? Of course not, we need to move pass the prejudice.

# Religion

I always felt fortunate to have been born in Chicago, Illinois and raised by parents who would have washed my mouth out with soap if I or my brothers uttered slurs about nationality, color or creed. Though politically conservatives, my parents raised us to be opened minded, fair and accepting of people based on their personal merit, and not because they were the "right" religion, color, from the "right" country of origin, or politically in agreement with us. Thank you Mom and Dad so very, very much.

When I was seven years old we moved to the village of Skokie, Illinois. There was a very large Jewish population, and many were WWII death camp survivors. There was also a very large German community. I figured folks from Skokie were Jewish, Lutheran, or Catholic. At the tender age of eight, I broke my parent's cardinal rule of behavior when I got mad at my best friend. In anger, I told her that Jews were responsible for killing Jesus Christ (I learned that at the parochial school I attended, so it must have been correct, right?). My friend ran home in tears and told her mother what I said. My parents' judgment and punishment were swiftly delivered. I have endeavored to never again repeat my ill-mannered and cruel behavior, and I learned a lifelong lesson about the importance of not causing pain to another through careless, thoughtless, ignorant behavior or speech.

Well, that's how it was within my childhood circle of influence. However, at the age of fifteen, I got a small taste of what it feels like to be on the receiving end of prejudice based on religion. I had a Jewish boyfriend who took me home to meet his mom and live-in grandmother. John introduced me as the girl he loved.

His mom gave an understanding smile, but his grandma started crying and wringing her hands. She ran from the room pulling at her hair and uttering epitaphs in Yiddish...I understood exactly what she meant even if I did not understand of what she said. Most of my neighborhood, buddies were Jewish. I got to know what was expected of young jewish men and women. They were expected to marry within their religion and traditions. I was a very blonde and blue eyed, a Catholic no less. Yeah, I understood her very well, and I did not blame her for her reaction. His grandma's only mistake was thinking I loved her grandson, as he professed to love me. He was very cute and unbelievably funny. But, I most certainly, had no long-term plans for him or anyone else. After all, I was only fifteen years old!

# Being Different

I was born into a family of three girls who were very fair, with green eyes and long blonde hair. I on the other hand had dark skin, dark hair and dark brown eyes. My sisters would tease me and tell me that I was adopted, and that that was the reason I didn't look like them or fit in. I was too young to realize that I took after my father who was an American Indian. In the family unit it was mainly just teasing that took place from my siblings. However, others outside of the family would make remarks that singled me out from my sisters. Remarks like: "wow, where did you come from" or "how did you end up with that dark hair with three blonde sisters?" If I had been an adult when asked these questions, it would have been simple to respond without giving any thought to the person being critical of me. But being a child, it made me feel as though something was wrong with me and it wasn't ok to look different.

To this day there is one thing from my childhood that still stands out, a portrait that was taken of the four of us girls. The photographer grouped the three of my sisters together and had me standing off to the side.

Authors Comment:

Children, sometimes by just being children in their innocent teasing and playing, can be hurtful and cruel to those who are different which can result in a loss of confidence and self esteem of those being taunted. Growing up with the thought of being different can change your view of the world and how you think of yourself.

# Facing Obstacles

I am a light skinned African American woman born 1939. Some may call me high yellow. As a very young child we (my parents and I) lived on a farm. This farm was owned by a white family and my father worked for them. There were other workers, who were white. My mother worked somewhere else, so my father would take me up to the boss's house where their daughter took care of me until my mother came to pick me up. I was 3 years old, I remember because my grandmother gave me three baby chickens on my birthday.

At dinner, the boss's wife cooked for all of the farm workers. My father and I were the only people of color at the dinner table. The lady, I do not remember her name, would turn a chair backwards so I could stand in it and eat.

After dinner her daughter would wash my face and hands and put me in this clean feather bed to take a nap. The daughter, Mack Ruth, would play her guitar and sing me to sleep. I never knew the differences in color at that time.

As I grew older and started school, children were quick to see my skin color and could be really mean. Most of the children at school had dark skin and let me know what color my skin was. I was called everything but black.

As I continued to grow, I learned that some people did not care for you because of your skin color.

Some white people treated you different because of skin color. But brown skinned children have called me half white and any other name they could think of.

I have experienced within the black race adults with very bad attitudes about color.

Skin color has never affected me in any way, because I know who I am and I like being me. Skin color does not make you different, personality, and attitude does.

We are children of a heavenly father, who loves us, no matter what color our skin is.

# What is Poor?

I had the privilege of growing up in a large family. To support this large family, my dad was in the Navy for 21 years. My Mom was a homemaker. We lived in a rented apartment in "city housing." It was a small town where everybody knew everybody. This, sometimes, was a disadvantage. I attended a catholic church/school from kindergarten through the eighth grade. Everyone wore uniforms. You would think that would be a good thing because no one could tell if you came from an affluent family or not. We were able to attend because my grandparents were involved with getting the church started and so my parents paid a reduced tuition rate.

Some of the other children's fathers were dentist, doctors, lawyers, council member, etc. One girl in my class told me I was a "nobody" because my dad was "just a sailor" and we were always going to be poor. The other children, the nuns and, unbelievably, even the priest always treated us differently. The nuns meant well but their kindness just exaggerated the fact that we did not have as much as the other children. Our school did not have a lunch program. Everyone brought his or her own lunch. I remember a lot of peanut butter and jelly sandwiches and occasionally some fruit and cookies. If anyone had any food they did not want, the nuns asked them to pass it to the end of the lunch table. After collecting the food, they would distribute it to the "less fortunate" children.

I really did not mind it. I knew they were just trying to be kind, but it just gave the other children more reasons to look down on us.

Once I overheard my parents talking and my mother was upset because of things the priest had said to her. When I went to him for my premarital interview, he told me I owed him, and if it were not for him I never would have gotten to go to that school. It was probably statements like that, that had upset my mother.

I did not mind wearing second hand clothes. However, it was embarrassing when someone would tell me I was wearing their old dress, blouse, or pants and then felt they had to tell everyone else. They would tell me I came from a poor family, and if people did not give me their old clothes I would not have any. I did not know what prejudice was and I am sure they didn't either; I just thought they were mean kids.

As an adult, I realize now that they were saying and doing such things because that was what they were hearing at home. Unknowingly, their parents were teaching them prejudice toward anyone who was "poor" according to their standards.

If you lived in "city housing," it is referred to as "the projects" now, you were labeled poor. We never thought we were poor. Growing up in "city housing" was great. There were always plenty of kids to play with. Many other military families lived there too. New kids were coming and going all the time. There was always a "Mom" around if you needed one in a hurry. Everyone was always ready and willing to help each other.

# Struggling With Identity

Throughout the years black people have struggled with their identity. If truth be told we all harbor feelings of some sort with the black/white issue. I know that I did. It took me years to come to terms with my identity as a black woman. Looking back, I remember things from my childhood that made me think of the type of negative image my lighter skinned sisters and I gave to our darker skinned sisters as children. I remember calling my sister Ruth black when I was angry with her. "You're black," I would say; we all did that to her. We would say black like it was some dirty word. The words were said to make her feel less than us and it made us, somehow, feel superior to her because we were lighter than her. Why did we do this? I never heard my parents say anything negative about darker skinned people.

My mother is a dark-skinned woman and my father was a very light skinned black man. Something had to have been programmed into our brains that to be a dark-skinned person was not the best thing. Well we all know that this programming started centuries ago in slavery by whites. Lighter skinned black slaves were usually the house slaves while the darker ones were mainly field hands. The house slaves were generally treated much better so naturally many of them probably felt a little bit better than the field hands. Many of the house slaves slept in the master's house even though it might have been on the floor from what I have read. But being on the floor in the "big house" was a lot better than being in the shacks with the field hands. So this programming began during that time and sadly has continued until this day.

We black people have had this self hatred syndrome going on inside of us for many years and some of us do not want to accept the fact that it still exist in some form even today. Who, especially nowadays, wants to believe that deep down inside we might actually hate being dark skinned? Or who wants to admit that deep inside they are actually glad that they are not dark skinned? Who wants to admit that deep down inside they have accepted the white man's standard of beauty? Who does in this age of Black Pride? When you have been programmed to think negatively about yourself, you can't just stop that type of thinking overnight. You didn't come by it overnight, it took years of conditioning.

Is it any wonder that some darker skinned black people might have resentment toward lighter skinned blacks? Is it any wonder that some lighter skinned black people feel superior to darker skinned black people? Considering our history, it shouldn't be. We should be done with this ill treatment of each other that pits us one against the other. We all are African American regardless of our skin color and to white people we are all just black folks. Negative thinking about our blackness has been embedded so deeply within us that we will act or say racist things about each other that we aren't aware we are saying or doing. Here is one example about myself which I am ashamed of.

I saw a little baby with extremely coarse hair and the first thing that came to my mind was that her mother will have to get her a relaxer quite early to straighten that out or she will not be able to comb it. Then I thought of course she could just get a good conditioner to soften the hair and make it easier for her to comb it. But why did I think of a relaxer first? It has to be that somewhere in my subconscious mind I am still thinking that straight-hair is better than coarse hair. This is just one incident and I can name others, but I think you get the picture.

I remember while growing up that all of the homecoming queens or prom queens were light skinned black girls, most with long hair. I don't recall seeing any dark skinned girl being named "Miss" anything growing up. But that has changed some now. Light skinned girls particularly the extremely light skinned ones, or as some people would call them "high yellow" were always thought of as being pretty whether they were or not. People were looking at their skin color and/or their hair length instead of how they actually looked. A dark-skinned girl had to be actually pretty before she was called pretty. She was naturally thought of as being unattractive because of being dark.

Growing up, there was a church that only had light skinned members. Darker skinned blacks were not allowed to attend.

There is a book written in 1971 called "Certain People, American's Black Elite, by Stephen Birmingham. In this book it explores the caste system among Blacks especially in regard to skin color, hair texture, and money. There are sororities and fraternities that had only very light skinned black people.

The movie "School Daze" by, Spike Lee hit upon that as well. There will be a movie out soon about so called "good hair." This is a problem that we still have within our race which is unfortunate.

I never had any negative experiences within my race because of my skin color. The prejudice that I experienced within my race growing up and as an adult has been because of class or social status. I have some very painful childhood memories of being treated differently by children and adults within my race because my family was poor. Children who were well off would laugh at our clothes. My sisters and I wore flour sack skirts to school. These were skirts made from emptied sacks of flour that our mother used when baking bread. The sacks came in different patterns; white with red or blue flower designs.

I went to play with a friend of mine one day whose family had money and her aunt came to the door and told me to go home and not to ever come back because her niece could not play with somebody like me. At a very early age I learned that to some black people if you did not have money you did not belong in their world.

As an adult my sisters and I attended a Presbyterian Church that had a white pastor. The church was filled with very high class black people…doctors, lawyers, engineers, etc. My sisters and I had good jobs working for the government so we naturally fit in. The church was located in the inner city although none of the members lived within the inner city. The pastor wanted to have vacation bible school and made the mistake of inviting the inner city children in the area. This came up in the planning committee for the vacation bible school. I will never forget the looks on the faces of some of the women on that committee. One of the women said: "we do not want those children in our church and around our children." My sister Ruth and I looked at each other in disbelief. We could not believe what we were hearing. The inner city children did not come. They were not good enough.

We left that church soon after that for more than one reason, but that alone was reason enough. I believe we have made tremendous gains toward learning to love ourselves more within our race. We still have a long way to go.

One of the things we have to come to terms with is to recognize that we may still harbor some prejudices within our subconscious. So when the ugliness of our own racist thoughts or actions comes to the surface, and they will, we must recognize them and deal with them.

# Life as a Chocolate Drop

Prejudice within your race.

I am 38 years old at the time of my contribution to this book. Honored to contribute to the work of my beautiful ivory and caramel aunt's work, I immediately traveled down memory lane to think of what life has been for me as a Dark Chocolate female in America. While traveling this road, I immediately felt some of the emotions which have impacted me so greatly because of the color of my skin: rejection, harshness, jokes, mocking, humiliation, pain, sadness, and pride.

It is important to understand the context of which I write regarding prejudice in my race. I was born in August of 1970, during a time when 'dark' was not socially accepted. Further, it was believed by many, even so-called Christians, to be a curse because of the sin of Cain. Therefore, within the Black race, anything that was "light, bright, and damn near white" was considered beautiful regardless of the reality. I am the darkest of all of my parent's children, all of my aunt's nieces, and of all of my cousins, even 2nd and 3rd generation. In my mind, this makes me quite special!

Although there was a drastic difference in my complexion and that of my cousins, as children, we were all very close and played together all of the time. However, I was often the butt of many painful jokes because of my dark skin. I know that my cousins, and other family never meant any harm but it left a lasting impression on my heart. I was called everything from 'tar baby' to 'blacky', even by my eldest brother. You see the jokes never stopped; home, school, community, church, and etc.

Kids often made fun of my dark skin saying that I was ugly because I was so black. It seemed that people got so caught up with my hair, the texture, and the length. It seemed to have been a shocker that my hair was 'good' but my skin was so dark. Well, I would often explain that my grandmother was a Black Indian and my biological grandfather was a White Indian. This 'acceptance of me' because of my hair impacted me in such a profoundly negative manner that I remember being excited at the first chance that I had to cut my hair short. In addition, I remember feeling that I would focus on the inside of a person because I knew in my heart that I was the most beautiful person in the world regardless of how people perceived me externally.

### How I moved beyond color within my race?

I am not sure that I ever really moved beyond color within my race. I am very conscious of it in all that I do. I mean, I have never been attracted to light complexioned males... always have I preferred very dark complexioned men. In my mind, these were the most beautiful and sexy individuals. I ask myself, is that wrong to be so partial to one physical feature of an individual?

Well, I don't know the answer, but tend to think that it places limitations on an individual…to only like White or only like Black or only like "Light Skinned" or only like "Dark Skinned" is a handicap and could cause one to miss a great opportunity for love.

Nevertheless, I believe that I have been able to move further beyond being handicapped by color because of the words that my mother spoke over my life, as a young child that her father spoke over her as a child. You see, Calvin White, my grandfather, was a very wise man! My mom often told me stories of how my grandfather told her that: "Baby, there will always be another person with prettier hair; a prettier face, or a prettier body."

"So you have to have beauty from the inside and know that you are beautiful from the inside and not focus on the outside person." My grandfather was one of a kind, loved by all! The irony of those words coming from my grandfather is that he was a very, very fair complexioned man who was bi-racial. He was simply amazing! My mother loved him dearly and so did all of my aunts, uncles, cousins, his employers, everybody.

In any event, hearing these stories from my mother strengthened me to deal with the harshness of the jokes that I received the majority of my life because of my dark skin. My mom, as a child, was a person of sayings. She would say to me, as far back as I can remember: "Your attitude determines your altitude!" So, I realized that the choice was mine…I could sit back and allow the pain of rejection to keep me in bondage or I could take it all in stride and move forward…I did the later; I chose to embrace the color of my skin as a attribute rather than a negative. I have been told by many that my outlook is odd and different.

While I don't disagree, I attribute it to my relationship with Jesus Christ, who my parents introduced me to at a very young age. You see, life is a box of chocolates and you just don't know when you are going to get chocolate on the inside or when you are going to get a nut. If people are allowed to control you and your outlook on life based on their perceptions of you and who you should be rather than what God made you to be, you will always be in hell! While my realization of this statement has been a very painful and difficult journey of realization, I am thankful for how it has helped me to prepare my daughter for a tough and grueling world.

"Colorism," (no it is not a real word) within the black race is a result of a larger issue of racism within this country. "Whitism," (not a real word either) defines who, what, when, and how the standard will be for individuals, business, and success in this country, the United States of America. Therefore, anything that does not resemble what "whitism" has defined is considered to be wrong; such as blacks and darker skinned people. This rejection of all else, falls down on every other race, gender, and class of people within and outside of the white race. To that end, there is no wonder that there is so much prejudice and colorism within the black race.

As it relates to the pain that I have encountered as a dark skinned female, it has been great and at a very early age. However, because of the strong foundation in Jesus Christ, I learned early that what man rejects can often be a blessing in strengthening and preparing you for a greater cause and plan for your life by God. I would rather be accepted by Jesus and rejected my man any day! To all of my sisters, regardless of your color, embrace who you are, who God made you to be!

Do not fall prey to becoming a particular size, skin tone, hair texture, hair length, or anything that can be taken away.

As long as your happiness and security is based upon something that can be removed, you risk being unhappy and insecure. Place your happiness and security in Him who made you and you are guaranteed to survive any storm that life throws your way or any tragedy meant for your destruction. Trust me; I speak these words from my heart and experiences not philosophy.

Respectfully submitted,

Marlo Thomas Watson

# Prejudice Within My Own Family

I find prejudice within my own family and peers a bit disturbing; if you do not think as does the majority then you are "a sell-out." When you don't frequent the hangouts in the gathering places or attend a mainstream church you are "strange." When you demand that your children and their children speak slower or use correct grammar then "you want to be white."

At half a century of age, I notice our younger children name-calling, using demeaning language, getting hung up on skin color when it's not "light or bright." Just last week my nephew made a comment to me as I was working in the yard: "You know you look like a slave with that head-scarf (bandana) on." I replied: "I am a slave, do you have a problem with the way I look?" "Well, yeah I do." He is only eleven years old. Our skin tones are not that much different, however, I am darker.

I find I will not get on the elevator alone with a black man who has his pants down below his butt with all his underwear hanging out. But then again, I would not get on the elevator with any young man dressed that way whatever his color.

I am truly amazed at my people. After being away for twenty years, I moved back to my home town and ran into an old acquaintance. My reply to the question: "How are you doing?" was up-beat, cheerful and honest. But I got the distinct impression, especially after a short silence, that if I had said I was not doing very well, it would have been a more acceptable answer. My doing well is of the Lord. When I am not doing so well, I am still doing well in spirit.

I visited a new church congregation and met an eighty-six year old lady. When I asked her how she was doing, she said: "I am blessed." Prior to meeting her, whenever I was asked how I was doing, I would always say: "I am wonderful." One day after giving my standard response, a passer-by stared at me and in a sarcastic tone said: "I've never met anyone who was wonderful." The old lady had told me: "Honey, there are days when you may not feel wonderful, but you are always blessed."

Often, when I am out and about, I will give a salutation – a hello or goodbye – in Spanish. So at a special group function, as I was going to my car, I said good-bye in Spanish to a group of young ladies getting into their car. One of them yelled out to me: "Speak to me like a N...r, not that s...t! Needless to say, I was blown away at her comment.

To me, prejudice has made us who we are today. We worked harder to achieve because we had to. I am proud to be Black in America.

# The Teacher

Detroit 2007, I don't know if this made the local news but a (sister) friend from Detroit  called me about a club promotion allowing all "light skinned" females free admission all night long into a club.  She and many more sister's were appalled and quickly came together to voice their distaste. By the time they were done, the promotion was cancelled.  Later we found out the club had also made plans for the following weekend for the dark skinned sisters.  How insensitive and uncaring some people can be.  Have we not learned anything over the last three hundred and ninety years?  We are now being divided by our own people for "thirty pieces of silver."  I am sure the club promoters have no prejudicial intentions, in mind but the results are still the same.  The last thing we need as a people, still struggling from the effects of slavery and its aftermath, is to be divided by color.

We know that slavery began in this country in 1619 as indentured servitude, but eventually evolved into the system we are all familiar with.  The lighter skinned slaves, because their color more closely resembled that of their masters, were usually employed in and about the house, and treated somewhat better than the darker field hand.

This disparity between the two classes of slaves caused in some cases resentment and dislike which, to a degree, is still manifested by people of color to this day. After the abolition of slavery, some of the former slave masters started a school and a community for the half white slaves. In the 1950s and 60s, a certain Black University ( a college at that time) in the south, was rumored to have mostly light-skinned females enrolled as apposed to their darker sisters.

There was a study conducted which showed that when it comes to hiring, if two blacks with the same credentials, are in contention for a job, in most cases the lighter skinned applicant will be the winner. This has gone on long enough. I no longer care how it got started; I just want it to end. I say to all my sisters and brothers, both light skin and dark, we cannot expect better treatment from others until we learn to love and respect ourselves. Then and only then, can we demand equal treatment with an equally clear collective racial conscious.

# A member of the white minority

I am a white male born in 1961 and the youngest of three children. My parents both came from rural Alabama. My mother's family had a large farm out in the country and raised all their own food, they never really needed much money since they raised everything themselves. My father's family resided in a small township surrounded by large cotton fields, my grandparents worked various jobs to provide for the family. My father joined the Army at age 16 so there would be one less mouth to feed and he could send money home to help the family. I tell you all this to give you some perspective of my parents' and family members views regarding race.

In Sept. 1967, I started 1st grade in the west Knoxville, TN suburb of Farragut. My family lived in a brand new split foyer house in the beautiful new suburban area. In November 1967 my family moved to Chattanooga, TN as it was more centrally located for my dad's work. Also, my paternal grandparents and two uncles and their families lived in Chattanooga. My dad moved us from the brand new split foyer home in the suburbs to a house nearly 70 years old in one of the older, inner city neighborhoods of Chattanooga called Highland Park. My grandparents lived right around the corner from us, so that was nice.

Highland Park was aging and changing fast at that time. The streets all ran east and west, or north and south, thereby creating many blocks with homes built close together by today's standards. All the blocks had sidewalks and streetlights, most homes didn't have garages for the cars, so people parked their cars on the street in front of their homes or in driveways in between the homes.

Highland Park was home to a large, very conservative Christian college which had a lot of married students who lived in the neighborhood with their families. Highland Park had several streets (blocks) where many black families lived. Highland Park had lots of white families that had not yet fled the neighborhood for the suburbs; these were hard working families like ours that had family ties to the neighborhood. Highland Park also had many older run-down homes that were inexpensive and many large old homes that had been carved-up into many cheap apartments. Many of the white families that lived in these rundown homes and cheap apartments had family members that didn't work, they collected disability or welfare, and usually drank their checks up before the month was over.

There was a very large old house across the street from ours that had been made into 4 or 5 apartments. We never saw the owner or even knew who the owner was. The residents had an old couch and kitchen chairs they kept on the front porch where they would sit outside in the evenings and drink. Their garbage cans usually overflowed with beer cans or liquor bottles from all they had consumed. The street in front of their house was thick with the solidified drippings of years of leaking oil from their old junker cars. The old house had a rotten metal roof, with collapsing gutters that actually had grass growing out of them. The top of the house was usually covered with pigeons. The old house must have had 3 or 4 chimneys (probably fallen in and no longer in working order) where pigeons would roost. My brother often shot pigeons off the roof of that old house with his pellet gun while sitting on our front porch, sometimes the dead pigeons would fall down into those chimneys!

I suddenly went from an all white, reasonably new, school in the suburbs to an inner city school at least 50 years old. I lived 3 houses beyond the zone to attend Highland Park Elementary where most of the white working class kids and children of the college students attended. I had to go to Hemlock Elementary which was near where the black families lived and attended school. There were also some other white kids, but not as many from the working class families, probably more from the lower class families I described previously. Also, some of the white kids in the neighborhood went to private schools, the Christian college had their own private elementary school and several churches in the area started small private schools when the city schools began bussing.

I would say that by the time I was in the 3rd grade, I was in the minority at Hemlock Elementary School. It was the same at the junior high and high schools I attended as well. I was a minority.

Both my parents and grandparents were employed. When my parents were going to be working when I got out of school, I would walk to the Boy's Club. I spent many hours at the Boy's Club, I loved it! I could play sports and games, they had a library and adult supervision, a snack bar to get something to eat or drink, they even took trips to see the Atlanta Braves or to the drag strip on occasion…..and it was cheap! The Boy's Club only cost $5 a year (what a bargain). My parents were satisfied with the Boy's Club as a place for me to go after school, instead of having to pay for some sort of after-school care program somewhere else. However, the Boy's Club was probably over 95% black by this time, maybe even 99%, so I was in the minority there as well.

This was my environment from the 1st grade to the 11th grade. In the 10th grade I began working at a grocery store after school, the grocery store was in a predominantly black area as well. Near the end of my 11th grade year my parents finally moved to the suburbs. But, as you can see, I lived and grew-up during my most "formative" years in this inner-city neighborhood as a minority at the schools I attended, the Boy's Club and playgrounds where I spent my time playing, and even at the grocery store where I got my first job. I certainly had numerous run-ins with some black males at school and at the boy's club, but I became good friends with other black males who watched out for me. We all tried to watch-out for each other and stay away from the troublemaking bullies that would take our snack money or any cash we happened to have on us.

As well as playing at the Boy's Club, I also spent many hours playing various sports on the playground at Hemlock Elementary. We (my friends and I) would play whatever sport was in season. I became a good athlete and was usually the first one to be chosen when we picked teams.

I was voted All-City in baseball in junior high and high school and was the only white "starter" my senior year on my high school's football team. I never let being in the minority prevent me from participating in anything I wanted to do.

I guess from growing up in this environment, I didn't develop the same racial views as other members of my family or many other white people for that matter. My parents were not openly racists, they didn't go around using the "N" word casually like so many white people did at that time. I do remember my father was a big supporter for George Wallace when he ran for President in1968. I also remember when I first realized my parents had racist views. I was in the 3rd grade and my friend Danny (who was black) was at my house playing. It was raining and we were playing on the front porch and we came up with the great idea that he should spend the night at my house. When I asked my mom if Danny could spend the night, she quickly said NO! Later she told me to never ask if Danny could spend the night again, he was black and that was not going to be allowed. She could not believe I even asked for Danny to spend the night with me. My mother actually liked Danny, but because of the racist views that she grew up with, it just wasn't going to happen.

It's funny how when we are kids parents don't think much about racial differences when kids play together (unless you ask if they can spend the night with you). I didn't really have any racial problems with my family or other white people until I got to be a teenager and began to enter puberty. Looking back on my life, it seems natural that I became interested in the black girls that were at the playground or the schools I attended, they seemed to pay more attention to me than any of the white girls that were around (and there were so few of them). This became a big problem for me at home with my family. I guess I was no longer a kid just having fun playing with my friends, I was now showing an attraction for the black girls in my environment, and many were attracted to me as well.

We had a 9th grade prom at the junior high school I attended. When I was in the 9th grade I was asked to go the prom by one of the prettiest girls in school, Peggy. Peggy lived a few blocks from me and also grew-up playing on the school ground with us as kids. I quickly agreed as I thought it was flattering to have such a beautiful date for the prom. As the prom got closer, I became afraid. What was I going to tell my family? Peggy was black and I knew my mother and father would not approve. Why had I agreed to go to the prom in the first place......I didn't even know how to dance!

As prom day got closer, my mom bought me a mint green leisure suit and a slick, silky printed shirt for the event. These were clothes that were in style at the time, whether you were white or black. The day of the prom I didn't know what I was going to do....could I ask my dad to stop and let me pick Peggy up like a date should? I tried to call Peggy and back out, she said if I could walk to her house her older sister would take us and pick us up. This was a great solution to my problem. I think my dad sensed what was going on, suddenly I didn't need a ride or even want him to drop me off or pick me up at school. I got dressed and walked the few blocks to Peggy's house and her sister took us to the prom and we had a great time. I can't recall if I actually ever danced to a song or not.

This was the first of many awkward situations that occurred when I didn't quite tell my parents the truth about some planned activity due to fear of their racial attitudes. It only got worse as I got older and had more and more interest in and from girls. I could not begin to count how many times I received a phone call from a black girl whom I knew from school or the neighborhood, only to have my parents berate me for the next hour as they believed they could tell the girl on the other end of the phone line was black. I would fire back that the girl called me; I did not call her....but my parents found that no more agreeable than if I had called the girl. There were times I actually closed myself up in a closet or crawled under the bed to get away from my parents and their harangues about race.

When I got to high school, I was mainly attracted to the black girls at school. My school a few years earlier had been majority white, and was known as the Rebels. They used to use the Confederate Soldier and flag as their mascot, but as whites fled further out to the county, the school became majority black. We were still known as the Rebels, but the school no longer used the Confederate soldier or flag as a mascot. However, there was a small group of white guys who didn't care for the changes in the school. They usually had Rebel flags in their car windows or on license tags and often started some sort of trouble with the black students. For some reason, these guys didn't seem to like me. I didn't know any of them and they didn't know me. We had not gone to elementary or junior high school together, but they seemed to pick-up on the fact that I had lots of friendships with many of my black classmates (many I grew-up with at the Boy's Club). This group often harassed me. They tampered with my motorcycle in the school parking lot (draining out my gas, unscrewing the idle screw, stealing my crash bars or mirrors).

My senior year I was elected as Most Popular and Mr. Brainerd High, but I didn't go to my prom. I was afraid of my family's reaction and the reaction of these other white students. I had my own car now and didn't have to worry about my dad carrying me, but what if they wanted to see pictures of the evening. It was just easier not to attend the big event....I was still nervous about dancing anyway!

As I completed high school and began college, I finally began to openly date the young black women whom I met at school or work and was attracted to. I continued to hide my dating from my family just so I would not have to listen to them.... it always came back to "you don't see red birds mixing with blue birds do you?" When I moved out of my parents' home at age 21, it became easier to hide my dating from my parents. However, on some occasions one of my brother's friends would see me out and tell my brother. My brother would tell my parents, and the next time I was at my parents' house I would be subjected to their vocal tirade.

When I was out about town with my date, I never tried to "hide-out" we would go to concerts or movies, just as others our age did. I never felt physically threatened while interracially dating, but we often did get stares as this was the late 70's and early 80's. Once while on a date at a concert, someone behind me threw a cup of soda on me. The folks behind us were white; no one said they were sorry, like it had been an accident. I've always guessed it was someone behind us that didn't agree with interracial dating and they threw the soda on me. We watched the entire concert; I didn't let it move me.

This brings me to the subject of this book...prejudice within your race. I don't guess it would be correct to say my parents were prejudiced against me, they just didn't agree with my views regarding race. They raised me, so why is it that my views of race differed from theirs? My guess is the environment in which I grew up played a large part, plus the fact my parents were not openly racist, they didn't walk around using the "N" word casually in their every day vocabulary like many white people did. I think my father was mainly concerned someone might hurt me for interracially dating, these were difficult times, and things were changing, but slowly. This was still the South, not New York or Los Angeles or other large cities where such things were common.

I guess I did experience prejudice or maybe just hatred, from other whites (not just my family) who saw me dating a black girl. So maybe I did experience prejudice within my race. I certainly saw and heard how racist whites could be when no African Americans were around. I never cared to be around people with such racist attitudes.

When I was 27 years old I fell in love with a beautiful young woman named Barbara who was "Bi-racial." Barbara's mother was from Germany (100% white) and her father's family came to New York from Trinidad (primarily of African descent). Barbara and I dated for about 7 months (still hiding such relationships from my family) before I decided I wanted to marry her. I knew my family would love her if they would only allow themselves to get to know her. I am glad to say I was right!!! My father immediately loved Barbara; my mother took a little more time. But as my brother married and divorced a couple times, my mother developed a great relationship with Barbara. Barbara would go to my mother to get my mother on her side if we had some sort of disagreement. My entire family truly loved Barbara....she healed a long cancer that had been in our family. I was finally at ease with my life and my family.

MAR 27 2004

74

# Inter and Intra Racial Prejudice

Dr. Shagufta Jabeen

"People say I talk, walk, behave, and want to be white. Some say I have dyed my hair light to look like them. I don't have control over my skin color which is light for my race and that's probably why I am seen as trying to be white. People comment that I am training my kids differently. I live in a metro area and am not able to go anywhere without getting criticism. I wanted to jog to get myself in better shape but it's not possible in my area, so where I can do that? I will be facing so many comments that I will go into post walk stress. Doc, why is this happening? We are in the 21$^{st}$ century; I want to adopt good things from others irrespective of their color."

"I am tired of living the life I have. There is a constant struggle with my in-laws beyond what most people face. I love my husband but my in-laws get in the way of caring for him. Intelligence is not a property of any race. With the high educational level my in-laws have (mostly doctors, engineers and MBAs); they should be above and beyond this prejudice. After all, we all carry the genes from one couple Adam & Eve.

If I ever choose to divorce my husband it will be because of them. Doc, please help me deal with this."

"I will not be able to live in this county anymore and I am feeling so depressed about it. My child goes to a school which is predominantly white and each day he comes back from school with a new comment, statement, or issue. I am now running out of explanations, for him. I can't answer his questions, of why, a person is judged by the color of their skin, or is there a machine or some kind of medicine that can change skin color? Doc, is there a way to help my growing child to get adjusted to this self created system?"


These are only a few examples of some of my patients who are going through a rough time because of the prejudice they have to face on a daily basis. These problems are at least partially responsible for their sufferings and their signs and symptoms of mental illnesses. Several have to take medication or undergo extensive psychotherapy to overcome or address these issues.

Inter and Intra racial prejudice is universal, ongoing, and has a destructive impact on our society. We all are the cause and effect of it. I don't think that there is a simple solution to it. I want to write a few things to highlight important issues in the form of questions, which frequently come to mind.

### What is the definition of a Race?

Race is defined as "a population with distinguishable biological features." Such characteristics are hair color and texture, skin color, eye color and shape, size of limb and body parts, and facial organs, etc. All these are outward expressions of the phenotypes of people.

## Why do humans have distinguishable biological features (base for the origin of racism/prejudice)?

All humans belong to the same species (Homo sapiens theory), and originated from one couple Adam & Eve. However, over a period of time changes in the selection of genes and their pairs, mutations in the genes and various combinations of offspring in each generation have led to distinguishing biological features of humans.

## How we got into this?

Scientists have reached the conclusion that these differences among people are superficial and a matter of gene selection. Furthermore, they agreed that all members of the species "Homo sapiens" have more characteristics in common than different. However, mankind continues to view each other from the features that are outwardly expressed which has led to what we call racial prejudice.

## What is Racial Prejudice?

Racial prejudice is an insidious moral and social disease affecting peoples and populations all over the world. It is diagnosed by its various symptoms and manifestations, which include fear, intolerance, discrimination, hatred, separation, and segregation.

## Why we have it?

As stated earlier, humans are outwardly different in appearance. Rather than embracing this difference and admiring the uniqueness of individuals who live in different parts of the globe, we start believing these differences separate individuals into groups, with one group being inferior to another.

**What is the cause of Prejudice?**

In a nutshell the single underlying cause of racial prejudice is ignorance.

Racism is moral blindness; it fails to appreciate that the difference in the biological and physical characteristics of individuals is a cause for wonder. Each race is unique; each individual is special. Most importantly, the differences are superficial. In reality, humans are largely more similar than different as supported by science and multiple Holy books. This provides evidence that all of mankind is of the same origin; Indeed we are one race of Homo sapiens. The diversity and uniqueness of the peoples and nations are manifestations of God's awesome creativity and power.

**Who has it?**

Racial prejudice affects everyone because people are "pre-judged" based on superficial characteristics. We can conclude that all people "suffer" from this on various levels. When we do not know an individual well, we consciously or unconsciously begin to characterize him or her based on what we see. Again, this is due to our ignorance of the person's real character and personality. We will form opinions, often based along stereotypical lines: "all people of a certain race are..." We can fill in the blanks with such expectations that certain races are intellectually superior, others are full or avarice, another is more artistically or athletically inclined, still another has members who are apt to be dishonest, and so on. These ideas have been formed from society, media, and our own upbringing.

These ideas may have been taught directly or indirectly. A child mimicking the behavior of his parents would be an indirect example. Whatever the source, even the most enlightened members of society will to some extent judge others based on the superficial aspects of race.

Indeed the problems arise when the symptoms of the disease become evident: intolerance, separation, and hatred.

**What is racism?**

Racism is the conviction that the members of one race are inherently superior to the members of other races. Thus, these groups deemed superior are allowed to gain economic power and social dominance over the other groups considered inferior. This conviction is often manifested by discriminatory or abusive behavior and practices towards the members of the supposed inferior races. Often the expectations and characterizations of one race concerning another are based on these prejudicial beliefs. Hence, racist individuals believe that members of certain races are prone to dishonest behavior, greed, aggression, immortal activities and promiscuous conduct.

Racism may also be characterized by other broad generalities such as the expectation that members of certain races are better athletes, more intelligent, have better voices or are more artistic.

While these characterizations are not necessarily negative, they still hold to a narrow view of certain populations. Racism is a limiting, narrow-minded mentality that does not allow one to judge another through knowledge and personal interaction.

Instead, an individual is judged solely by the racial or ethnic group they belong to. In actuality, racist individuals are virtually incapable of any fair or correct evaluation of another person. Racial prejudice builds a wall. It is impossible to see past the preconceived ideas.

Racism has birthed many of society's ills. Discrimination, separation, and segregation are products of a racist mentality. Forced slavery and genocide are capital crimes directly resulting from racism. When one race acts out its superior beliefs in a society, there is no room for harmony or community. In order to remain superior, members of one race have enslaved and/or destroyed their "neighbors."

## What are the emotional outcomes?

Often underlying racial prejudice and racist beliefs is the emotion of fear. Many individuals react with fear towards those who look or appear different. Fear leads to self-protectiveness and defensiveness mostly causing pain and discomfort to the object of the fear. Instead of attempts to bridge the differences, the wall is maintained; unity and harmony are never reached.

Anger, frustration, depression, anxiety, and to extreme cases psychosis may result with accompanied indulgence in drinking or using drugs as a method of self treatment or physiological sufferings such as poor sleep, appetite, energy level, incapability to concentrate and focus, headache, fluctuations of blood pressure, hormonal abnormalities and so much more.

A sense of being under constant surveillance by others makes a person uncomfortable at any situation, leading to constant vigilance and keyed up behavior. Muscle tension, irritability, mood swings, and anger out burst are common sequels. Acute or chronic victimization may lead to very intense emotions, which may result in violent acts such as sociality, aggravated assaults or even homicides.

**What are implications on Societies?**

Racial prejudice has shaped the form of our present day societies; indeed, prejudice has shaped societies since time began. As far back as the children of Abraham, Isaac, and Jacob living in the lad of Goshen, people have been subjugated due to their differences. Wherever there are differences, there is fear, intolerance, and injustice.

Racial prejudice has affected schools, homes churches, work places, shopping places, public transportations, police/jails/prisons, virtually any place or situation which brings two people together. **The effects of racism can be witnessed at a political, socioeconomic, community, and family level.**

The wars have shaped up religions and countries and the prejudice has taken a form not only against a race but country, region, or subcontinent. To counteract the disease of racial prejudice, modern-day societies have drafted and enacted legislation to ensure that people "treat" each other with respect and dignity allowing one another their inalienable right to their pursuit of life, liberty, and happiness. While man's actions can be legislated, their hearts and fears cannot. Thus, society continues to suffer from the disease. Forums, coalitions, and initiatives continue to be formed to foster unity, understanding, and tolerance.

### Is racism an international issue?

Racial prejudice is a matter of growing concern amongst the nations of the world. Far from being a social illness restricted to one or two countries, the moral disease spans communities, countries, and continents. It is a complex issue. It exists not only among different races but also interestingly among members of the same race. Over the years, peoples and nations exhibiting higher degrees of civilization have been deemed racially superior.

Mankind has been unable to embrace and celebrate the uniqueness of the various ethnic groups. Instead, fear has taken control. Xenophobia, defined as an intense fear and dislike of foreign people, or simply racial intolerance, is a disease reaching epidemic proportions.

Traditionally, ethno-national conflicts had to do with struggling over resources and land possession. Often these conflicts were tied to religious intolerance. More recently, globalization has added to this situation; trade and commerce between the nations aided by modern-day technology has increased the interaction of foreign peoples with one another. Anti-immigration has become part of the political debate in countries worldwide, especially in Europe; the outcome of many elections had hinged upon this question.

Racism has unfolded in every continent. In Europe, extreme racist groups have gained more and more acceptability in countries like France, Germany, and Austria. In Australia, the Aborigines have lost much of their land and have been the victim of extreme prejudice. Not only has Apartheid, legalized separation, been practiced in Australia, it has been a well-publicized condition in South Africa. Many African countries have endured long-term civil wars, some beginning shortly after that nation's freedom from former colonial countries.

In Asia, Cambodians harbor extreme prejudices against the Vietnamese, and Chinese students have been forbidden access to higher education in Malaysia. In the Middle East, antagonism between the Israelis and the Palestinians continues to exist.

## What is the state of race relations in 21st Century America?

America has had a long history of racism. Racism has infiltrated every aspect of American society and shows no sign of decreasing. This fact is more easily understood if racism is viewed for what it really is at its core: an institutional ideology. It is a misunderstanding to equate racism with the evil-minded treatment of one individual to another. Racism is more than just personal hatred.

Racism is allowed to subsist because it is fostered and maintained by institutions and government. Even if individuals within groups or members of a corporate hierarchy determine that the practices of a particular institution are racist, those individuals would be hard pressed to bring about change.

When seeking to understand the state of race relations in 21st Century America, one must gain a clear picture of the nature of racism; it is the belief that one group of people with a particular biological make up is superior to other groups with a differing biological make up. This condition is all the more exasperating in America because of the many strides that have been made over the past decades to combat the situation.

In those earlier days in the 20th century, the face of racism was largely black and white. Today, the face of racism has become multi-colored and multicultural. With the high increase of diverse populations entering and maintaining communities all over the country, racism has expanded to include antagonism between peoples of many cultures.

The 21st Century has brought about many attempted changes in society. There is legislation and memoranda against discrimination in its many forms. Affirmative action has been used as an attempt to ensure individuals are given equal opportunity for employment, housing, and other types of advancement. Television shows have changed format and characters to seek political correctness. Nevertheless, society cleverly and subtly maintains its separate views of the races. Ancient barriers, though invisible, still exist owing to the unhappy truth that it is still impossible to legislate the hearts of men. There will always be those who will fight for change while others resist, seeking to maintain the status quo. These are issues of economy, power, and control not easily relinquished. Inasmuch as racism is an institutional ideology, there can still be no improvement unless many individuals work towards it.

## What is the solution?

As prejudice is a complex and multifactorial issue, the solution is not going to be an easy one. There has to be various levels and check points starting from individuals themselves to societies at large. Education can play a significant role. Although there is always a bright side of strive for, this intricately complex issue may remain throughout the existence of mankind.

Dr. Shagufta Jabeen
Meharry Medical College
Department of Psychiatry
& Behavioral Science
Nashville, Tennessee

# Epilogue

My sister and I wrote a book together about our father entitled: "The Man Behind the Name." We wanted to share his story with others and after writing about our father we realized we had more stories to tell. While discussing some of the events that had occurred in our lives, we realized that each of us had encountered quite a bit of racial bias, which by itself, is not unusual in the lives of African-American people. But the more we reminisced, the more we recalled incidents collectively and separately of bias and prejudice coming from people of our own race. So we wondered how many other people had experienced this and "Bingo," we had our topic, "Prejudice within Your Race."

After reading Sunshine's story, do you think she has come to terms with who she really is as a person?

Are you dealing with conflicts of your own and if you are how have you dealt with them?

After reading these stories, has it helped you come to terms with some of the struggles, or did it provide answers for you?

How surprised were you when you read that in 2008 we are still struggling with the same old issues?

Are you now more sympathetic to others of another color after reading this?

What makes people act differently to people who look and act differently than they do?

Children become what they hear and see, weather it is negative or positive. They most often, emulate their parents, but it behooves us all to be good examples for them. As parents, we must teach our children to respect and embrace those who are different, learn from and share this world with all mankind.

# Notes

# Notes

# Notes

# Notes

# Notes